Clown's Party

Written by Jill Eggleton
Illustrated by Craig Smith

A party!
Come to a party
on Saturday.
2 Jack Street.

"Look!" said Clown.
"I am going to a party!"

Clown went into the shed.

"Look at my car," said Clown. "No wheel!"

"I am **not** going
in my car,"
said Clown.

"I am going on my bike."

"Look at my bike," said Clown. "No seat!"

"I am **not** going on my bike," said Clown.

Clown went into the house.

He looked
in the cupboard.

"Look!" said Clown.

"Look at my skates!"

"I **am** going to the party," said Clown.
"I am going on my skates!"

Party Invitations

Guide Notes

Title: Clown's Party
Stage: Early (1) – Red

Genre: Fiction
Approach: Guided Reading
Processes: Thinking Critically, Exploring Language, Processing Information
Written and Visual Focus: Invitations
Word Count: 85

THINKING CRITICALLY
(sample questions)
- What do you think this story could be about?
- Look at the title and read it to the children.
- Why do you think there is no wheel on Clown's car?
- What do you think might have happened to the seat on Clown's bike?
- Do you think it was a good idea for Clown to go to the party on skates? Why/why not?
- How else do you think Clown could have gone to the party?

EXPLORING LANGUAGE

Terminology
Title, cover, illustrations, author, illustrator

Vocabulary
Interest words: skates, shed, cupboard
High-frequency words: looked, into
Positional words: into, on, in

Print Conventions
Capital letter for sentence beginnings and names (**C**lown), full stops, commas, exclamation marks, quotation marks